COYOTES

by Sandra Lee

The Child's World®

Content Adviser:
The Zoological Society
of San Diego

Published in the United States of America by The Child's World®
PO Box 326 • Chanhassen, MN 55317-0326
800-599-READ • www.childsworld.com

PHOTO CREDITS
© Altrendo Nature/Getty Images: 24–25
© Bill Lea/Dembinsky Photo Associates: 7
© Charles Mauzy/Corbis: 16–17
© Daniel J. Cox/naturalexposures.com: cover, 1
© E. R. Degginger/Dembinsky Photo Associates: 5
© George D. Lepp/Corbis: 19
© Joe McDonald: 14–15
© Michael DeYoung/Corbis: 20–21
© Nicholas DeVore/Getty Images: 13
© Randy Wells/Corbis: 8
© W. Perry Conway/Corbis: 10–11, 22–23, 26–27

ACKNOWLEDGMENTS

The Child's World®: Mary Berendes, Publishing Director;
Katherine Stevenson, Editor

The Design Lab: Kathleen Petelinsek, Design and Page Production

LIBRARY OF CONGRESS CATALOGING-IN-PUBLICATION DATA
Lee, Sandra, 1940—
  Coyotes / by Sandra Lee.
    p. cm. — (New naturebooks)
  Includes bibliographical references and index.
  ISBN 1-59296-634-9 (library bound : alk. paper)
  1. Coyote—Juvenile literature. I. Title. II. Series.
  QL737.C22L45 2006
  599.77'25—dc22   2006001361

Table of Contents

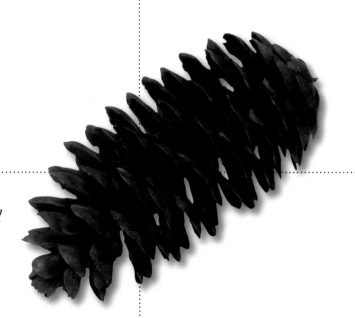

On the cover: This coyote is resting in the sand in Utah's Little Sahara area.

Meet the Coyote!

The official name for coyotes is *Canis latrans*, which means "barking dog" in Latin.

It is late at night, and the southwestern desert is still. The stars are sparkling in the clear night air. You crawl into your tent and snuggle down in your sleeping bag. Soon you are drifting off into a deep sleep. Suddenly, you are awakened by a long, sad howl. Other voices join in, and the night comes alive with a chorus of barks, yaps, and howls. What animals are making these mournful sounds? They're coyotes!

This coyote is howling on a moonlit night. Do you think it is sending out the first howl or answering another coyote's call?

What Do Coyotes Look Like?

Coyotes are also sometimes called "brush wolves."

An adult coyote can weigh up to 40 pounds (18 kg) and stand about 25 inches (64 cm) high at the shoulder.

It's no surprise that coyotes are members of the dog family. With their slender legs and bushy tails, coyotes look a lot like the dogs we keep as pets. A full-grown coyote is about the same size as a small collie. Coyotes are closely related to wolves, foxes, and jackals. Sometimes coyotes are called "prairie wolves."

Coyotes are very curious animals. This coyote is concentrating on something across a field of snow—it isn't even paying attention to the photographer taking its picture.

A coyote's face is very expressive. It can show fear, curiosity, and affection, just like a dog's. Coyotes also have very good hearing. They aim their pointed ears in the direction of sounds they find interesting. They can hear the slightest sounds—even a mouse under the snow. A coyote's sense of smell is excellent, too.

Coyotes are very clever animals. In fact, the world "coyote" comes from the Aztec word coyotl, which means "trickster."

An angry coyote holds its tail straight out from its body. This lets other coyotes know that it's upset and that they should stay away.

It's not difficult to figure out how this coyote feels! It's snarling at another coyote that has come too close to its meal.

Where Do Coyotes Live?

Like other members of the dog family, coyotes can't sweat. To keep cool in warm weather, they must breathe in short, rapid breaths. This kind of breathing is called panting.

Coyotes are intelligent animals that can adapt to all kinds of conditions. They live throughout the United States and Canada, from the mountains of Alaska to the deserts of Arizona. Some even live in canyons near the city of Los Angeles! Coyotes also live as far south as Central America.

To live in so many different places, coyotes must be able to survive in a wide range of **climates**. Those that live in northern climates have thicker fur that protects them from the cold. Their fur is often lighter-colored to help them blend in with forest areas and plants. Coyotes that live in desert areas have reddish-brown or gray fur that blends in with the mountains and sand.

This coyote lives in Colorado. It is searching for mice among the rocks and shorter grasses of a field.

What Do Coyotes Eat?

Coyotes may spend up to 30 minutes tracking their prey before attacking.

Coyotes eat lots of different things. Their main food, or **prey**, seems to be **rodents** such as mice, gophers, and prairie dogs. Coyotes eat fruit, birds, frogs, bugs, toads, and snakes, too. Coyotes will also eat **carrion**, or animals that are already dead.

Though coyotes prefer to live alone, they sometimes get together in small groups, or **packs**, to hunt and feed. Sometimes lone coyotes even hunt with badgers! The coyote uses its keen sense of smell to find a rodent tunneling beneath the ground. Then the badger digs up the animal with its powerful claws. The coyote and the badger then share the meal.

Here you can see an adult coyote as it chases a mouse near Jackson Hole, Wyoming. After coyotes kill smaller prey such as mice, they often play with their kill before they eat it. They might pick up the dead animal with their teeth and toss it into the air. Other times coyotes will bat at their prey with their front paws.

In times when their main food is scarce, small coyote packs may attempt to hunt bigger animals such as elk, deer, or antelope. They chase these animals in relays, with one coyote taking over after another gets tired. The large animal eventually becomes too tired and weak to fight off the whole group. The coyote pack can then attack and share the meal.

Coyotes that live in or near city areas have been known to eat anything from garbage to small housepets!

This coyote is standing near a deer that its pack just killed.

Coyotes can run very fast—up to 40 miles (64 km) per hour. That's faster than the speed limit for cars in some cities! Despite their speed, coyotes aren't big enough to kill healthy deer. The only large animals they can catch are usually those that are sick or dying. After eating, the coyotes gather for a long howl before going their separate ways.

When they run, coyotes carry their tails low to the ground. Wolves carry their tails higher—at the same level as their backs.

These coyotes are feeding on an elk in Yellowstone National Park.

17

Why Do Coyotes Howl?

Coyotes can make up to 11 different sounds. They howl, growl, bark, wail, and even squeal.

Scientists believe that coyote sounds mean different things. Coyotes seem to yelp when they are happy. They bark to threaten something or to protect themselves or their pups. To quietly call their pups, they make a "huff" sound.

Howling often begins with just a short bark or yap. This soon turns into a long yell. After a minute or two there is a pause, and then the coyote begins again.

No one knows for sure why coyotes howl, but many people think they howl to communicate. Coyotes might howl to show that they are lonely or sad. They might howl to let other coyotes know where they are or where they have claimed a **territory**. Coyote packs might howl together after a big meal to celebrate finding food. Scientists are still puzzled, but they are trying to learn more.

Coyotes, wolves, and dogs throw their heads back when they howl. Often, they shut their eyes as if they are singing a serious song.

What Are Baby Coyotes Like?

Sometimes coyotes use dens left behind by other animals, such as badgers.

Coyotes might use the same den for several years.

Coyotes are very good parents. They mate and stay together for years. Baby coyotes are born in the spring. Their mother makes a **den**, which is often a hole or tunnel dug into the ground. The newborns stay in the den, safe from enemies. The parents sleep outside, curled up beside a bush or a rock. If they sense danger, the parents move the pups to a new den.

These three coyote pups are watching the forest from the edge of their den.

Usually the mother has a **litter** of two to 12 pups. She nurses the pups with milk from her body for about a month. Then the pups are old enough to eat solid food.

At mealtime, the pups come out of the den to eat. The mother stands nearby, watching for danger. The father brings the pups food. He eats something, such as a rabbit, then comes home and spits up the food in front of the pups. It doesn't sound very tasty to us, but to the pups it's baby food—little chewing is needed!

This coyote mother and her pups live in Colorado. The pup on the right is trying to get its mother to spit up some food. To get their parents to spit up, pups nudge their noses into the corners of their parents' mouths.

Coyote pups don't open their eyes until they are about eight days old.

Out of every 10 coyote pups, often only two will survive their first year of life.

Like other puppies, young coyotes play with one another and with the adults. Their favorite games are tag, hide-and-seek, and nip-and-run. These games teach the coyotes skills they will need for hunting and for protecting themselves. The adults teach the young coyotes how to howl. In the fall, the pups go off to raise families of their own. Some of the young females might stay with the parents and form a pack.

Coyote parents sometimes bring their pups live mice for hunting practice.

These two coyote pups might look as though they are fighting, but they are actually playing.

Are Coyotes Pests?

Wolves and coyotes often compete for food. The numbers of wild wolves have dropped because of hunting and other problems, while coyote numbers have risen.

Unfortunately, coyotes have some habits that make them unpopular with farmers. Sometimes they raid fields of ripe watermelons. Though they take only a bite or two out of each melon, they can destroy an entire crop.

Many ranchers who raise sheep and other **livestock** also dislike coyotes. They often blame coyotes for killing their animals. Actually, coyotes help the ranchers. They kill rodents and rabbits that eat the same foods as the livestock. If they can find plenty of rodents, coyotes seldom bother farm animals.

This coyote is carrying a vole it just caught on a Kansas farm. Voles are also called "meadow mice." They are pests to farmers because they eat everything from crops to garden plants.

Do Coyotes Have Enemies?

Coyotes swim very well—but only when they have to.

Wild coyotes often live to be about eight years old.

Sometimes large **predators** such as wolves, grizzly bears, or cougars attack coyotes. Humans, however, are their greatest enemies. Some federal and state programs try to control the number of coyotes. When a single coyote causes problems for people living in an area, **game wardens** try to solve the problem by getting rid of just that animal. Even with all the dangers coyotes face, they keep surviving and finding new places to live.

The next time you hear the far-off howl of a coyote, listen—do other coyotes join in? What do you think they are saying to each other? Perhaps one day, you'll discover a way to find out!

This coyote is howling as the sun sets over a canyon in Mexico.

Glossary

carrion (KAR-ree-yun) Carrion is dead animals. Coyotes sometimes eat carrion.

climates (KLYM-etz) Climate is the type of weather an area has. Coyotes live in many different climates.

den (DEN) A den is an animal's home. Coyotes live in dens, often underground.

game wardens (GAYM WARD-enz) Game wardens are people who enforce laws having to do with animals and wildlife.

litter (LIT-ter) A litter is a group of babies born to one mother at the same time. Coyote litters usually have between two and 12 pups.

livestock (LIVE-stok) Livestock are animals raised on a farm. Cows, pigs, and sheep are livestock.

pack (PAK) A pack is a group of animals. Coyotes sometimes travel in small packs.

panting (PANT-ing) Panting is breathing in short, rapid breaths. Coyotes must pant to keep cool.

predators (PRED-uh-terz) Predators are animals that hunt and eat other animals. Coyotes are predators.

prey (PRAY) Prey animals are animals that are hunted and eaten by other animals. Mice are common prey for coyotes.

rodents (ROHD-ents) Rodents are animals with large front teeth used for chewing and nibbling. Squirrels and mice are rodents.

territory (TEHR-ih-tor-ee) A territory is an area in which an animal lives, hunts, and raises its babies. Adult coyotes have territories.

To Find Out More

Watch It!

Yellowstone: Realm of the Coyote. VHS. Washington, DC: National Geographic Video, 1995.

Read It!

Barrett, Jalma. *Coyote.* Woodbridge, CT: Blackbirch Press, 2000.

Morgan, William. *Navajo Coyote Tales.* Santa Fe, NM: Ancient City Press, 1988.

Swanson, Diane. *Coyotes.* Milwaukee, WI: Gareth Stevens, 2002.

Taylor, Harriet Peck. *Coyote Places the Stars.* New York: Bradbury Press, 1993.

Winner, Cherie. *Coyotes.* Minneapolis, MN: Carolrhoda Books, 1995.

On the Web

Visit our home page for lots of links about coyotes:
http://www.childsworld.com/links

Note to Parents, Teachers, and Librarians: We routinely check our Web links to make sure they're safe, active sites—so encourage your readers to check them out!

31

Index

About the Author

Sandra Lee began her career as a high school English teacher. After leaving teaching, she became an editor of children's books. Her interest in writing and love of reading inspired her to become an author herself. Sandra especially loved writing Coyotes because she lives in the California desert and hears the coyotes howling nightly. Sandra's favorite role in life is being a grandmother and dog owner.